The Poetic Voice

DR. IAN PRATTIS

Manor House

Library and Archives Canada
Cataloguing in Publication

Title: The poetic voice / Dr. Ian Prattis.
Names: Prattis, J. I., author.
Description: Includes bibliographical references.
Identifiers: Canadiana 20240480597 |
ISBN 9781998938148 (hardcover) |
ISBN 9781998938131 (softcover)
Subjects: LCGFT: Poetry.
Classification: LCC PS8631.R396 P64 2024 | DDC C811/.6—dc23

Cover Art: The Bay: Carolyn Hill
Cover design and interior layout: Michael Davie
Published in 2024 by Manor House Publishing Inc.
452 Cottingham Crescent, Ancaster, ON, L9G 3V6
905-648-4797 – All Rights Reserved.

Description:
"This book is based on my life experiences with humanity and nature. Relying on wisdom gained via teachings from First Nations and other spiritual traditions, I've journeyed through dark times into love and light. Through my experiences I hope the reader can see glimpses of themselves and touch the emotional connection with their own spirit." - **Dr. Ian Prattis**

"*The Poetic Voice*... encapsulates a wonderful life, a journey of mindfulness, difficulty, joy and love. Ian's connection with the Indigenous, with nature, and his own avatar mortality is what we'll remember as a legacy that should impact generations to come." **- Claudiu Murgan**, editor, *Love Letters to Water*

Funded by the Government of Canada

FOR CAROLYN HILL

A poet drives a furrow

never straight

as an eagle soars in a sky

without horizon or meter.

Cascading into passages that hover,

tracing cosmic runes

at the edge of knowing.

The Muse –

Waiting, wondrous,

for cracks

in façade's order to crumble.

Then she grants her life to a poem.

ACKNOWLEDGEMENTS

This was a difficult book to write. The form travelled from my childhood to being an elder of over 82 years. I think of my students at Carleton University in Ottawa and dedicate my last work to them.

I wrote worthwhile books as *Redemption* got Gold at the 2015 Florida Book Award. *Trailing Sky Six Feathers* received the 2015 Quill Award. *Failsafe: Saving the Earth from Ourselves* got the Silver for Environment. In 2019 *Our World is Burning* received eLit Excellence Awards. I received the 2011 Ottawa Earth Day Environment Award and in 2018 the Yellow Lotus award from the Vesak Project for spiritual guidance and teaching dharma. Ottawa Independent Writers have published my short stories in their anthologies.

Indigenous First Nation elders taught me the ways and traditions to guide my way onwards. They knew the genocide they suffered was at the hands of clergy, colonialists and industrialists – stamped into their brains and hearts.

As a university professor I had the privilege of experiencing thousands of student dialogues. I created the Dr. Ian Prattis Scholarship for Indigenous, Black and Racialized students at Carleton University. I provide an annual value of $2,000 every year for this scholarship.

The poems and chapters in this book become as seeds in the mind of the reader, so my work cannot be lost.

I thank Bob Barclay and Mark Rossi for their belief in my work.Thank you Suha Mardelli, Claudiu Murgan, Jana Begovic, Koozma Tarasoff, Krystina McGuire-Eggins, Lynn Adamson-Malelli, Carol Gravelle, Dawn James, Peggy Lehmann, Shobha Gallagher, Carolyn Hill, Judith Matheson, Iain Prattis, Alex Prattis, Nancy Brown, Romuald Dzemo and Grandmother Gayle Crosmaz.

My thanks also to publisher Michael Davie and Manor House for releasing my work to a world audience.

ABOUT THE AUTHOR

Ian Prattis, a poet and scholar, peace and environmental activist, was born on October 16, 1942, in Great Britain. Ian grew up in Corby, a tough steel town populated by Scots in the heartland of England's countryside. Ian was an outstanding athlete and scholar at school, graduating with distinctions in all subjects and was top graduating student. He did not stay to collect graduating honours, as at seventeen years old he travelled to Sarawak, Borneo, with Voluntary Service Overseas (1960–1962) - Britain's Peace Corps.

Returning to Great Britain after Sarawak was an uneasy transition. He did, however, manage to stumble through an undergraduate degree in anthropology at University College London (1962–1965), before continuing with graduate studies at Balliol College, Oxford (1965–1967).

At Oxford, academics took a back seat to the judo dojo (where he earned a University Blue), rugby field, bridge table and the founding of irreverent societies at Balliol. Yet by the time he pursued doctoral studies at the University of British Columbia (1967–1970), his brain switched on. He was a Professor of Anthropology and Religion at Carleton University in Ottawa from 1970 to 2007 and has worked with diverse groups all over the world. His highly acclaimed television course on "Culture and Symbols" drew on his novel perspectives. His millennium project for the year 2000 created another twelve-part television course on "Ecology and Culture." This educational enterprise produces a cadre of environmental activists each year.

He has trained with Masters in Buddhist, Vedic and Shamanic traditions and travelled widely on this beautiful planet, giving talks and retreats in Canada, India, Europe, the USA and South America. The basic commitment he holds is to make the world a beautiful place by encouraging people to embrace their true nature. His teaching focused on the spiritual issues of the day and honors all traditions.

His interests include cross-country skiing, hiking, canoeing and caring for the world of nature. He also enjoys Qi-Gong, gardening, playing baseball and swimming with dolphins. Ian lives with his wife Carolyn in the west end of Ottawa. This is Ian's twenty – first book. He continued to write books after retiring from Carleton University. He has authored books on dharma, on the environment, poetry and novels. He enjoys the freedom to create at his own pace. He has yet to discern the ordinary meaning of retirement!

TESTIMONIALS

"The Poetic Voice" by Ian Prattis is a collection of poems that are thematically arranged to the very soul of humanity, filled with imagery and rhythms. This poet succeeds in capturing moments of reality that allow readers to connect with what he writes about. The voice is powerful, the poetic lines of rhythmic and the entire collection is filled with graceful imagery.... The author articulates brilliantly on a variety of themes between humanity and nature... You will read these poems and go back to read them again and again!"
- **Romuald Dzemo**, Readers Favorite

"Your work is a beautiful synopsis of how you create what is around you. Starting with kind words for your rock – your beautiful wife and ending with your new poems. In between with work encompassing your life's work. Totally lovely – so much love that we all get it!"
Krystina McGuire-Eggins, Therapist

"Every poem written in this creation by Dr. Ian Prattis created a vivid painting in my mind. As an artist I could see his words splashed across the canvas with my brush. Connecting the energies of Mother Earth and the wisdom of the First Nations people brought me home to myself. Ian's positive influence on his students' greater purpose in life is assured. My ancestors brought him into my life several years ago, which has forever changed my path ahead. His watchful eye on my own struggles and adventures guided me to be safe and aware. Dr. Ian Prattis is not only a magnificent collector of thoughts and words he is a man of honour and beauty."
- **Gayle Crosmaz**, White Raven/Black Bear/Shaman

"Ian is my cousin, my mother's favorite nephew. He left our familiar space language in his youth, to higher ground from which to survey this wide world and study everything within it! He lived and learned. With experience comes wisdom and an occasion to inspire poetry. The collected of his poems capture Ian's respect for our Mother Earth in all of her beauty. They unveil the shadows and sunlight of his deep psyche and the peaks and valleys of his fortune. Above all, Ian's words reveal the great love in his heart, which he shares with every soul he touches. We are all born and we will die. It is our challenge to fill the "in-between" with the poetry of life. Ian is doing it all in spades."
- **Lynn Adamson–Malelli**, Author, Artist

"The verses of *The Poetic Voice* tell a story about life. From the boldness of youth to the quiet wisdom of senior years, Ian Prattis describes the human condition. Through life experience, connection and love the transcendent spirit evolves. Reading through these pages we see a glimpse of ourselves."
- **Peggy Lehmann**, Author, Editor

"Words are scarce to describe the feelings stirred by reading *The Poetic Voice*. It encapsulates the culmination of a wonderful life, a journey of mindfulness, difficulty, joy and love. Ian's connection with the Indigenous, with nature, and his own avatar mortality is what we will remember as a legacy that should impact generations to come."
- **Claudiu Murgan**, Author-editor, *Love Letters to Water*

TABLE OF CONTENTS

PART ONE:
Wedding Song

I do not have the credentials to speak of this Wedding Song. My relationships through time hardly equipped me, as I stumbled through ignorance, stupidity (mostly mine) and unhappiness. My mistakes were legion and I eventually decided to live alone.

I found a spacious cabin set in the Gatineau Forest across the river from Ottawa, in Quebec. Mother Nature held me, First Nations medicine people helped me transform childhood trauma. Slowly I came into balance, yet remained reclusive. I tried ballroom dancing, noticed an attractive blonde woman always dancing the male part with her female friends. Her name was Carolyn. I asked if she would like to dance the female role with me. Her wide green eyes and gentle smile said it all. The following week of dancing with her was magic. Not once did I tread on her toes during the intricate passages of the Quick Step and Fox Trot.

Before leaving that evening, I asked if she would like to meet my wolf. As soon as these words came out of my mouth, I thought she must think this was the worst pick-up in the world.

She paused, smiled and then said "Yes." I rolled down the window of my truck and Carolyn could see his magnificence. I should have called him "Hollywood Joe" instead of the rather lame "Wolfie" name I gave to him. He had a russet brown coat with white forelegs and face. He rested his large paw on Carolyn's shoulder and gently licked her cheek. It was an instant match. She told me much later that she fell in love with the wolf first, then thought that there must be something about the fellow who had him.

Carolyn's composure, presence and beauty opened me in a way never before experienced. There was a quiet purity to her being. I had the sharp realization that I would never meet anyone else like her. This was new and quite overwhelming.

We were married in a Buddhist monastery in France on July 21, 2001, after spending an extraordinary decade together. France was overflowing with friends drawn from all over the world. We had prepared our individual vows.

Carolyn insisted on going first. She did not speak her vows, she sang them. Her beautiful voice resonated through the temple. There was not a dry eye amongst those gathered – and that included me. It took a while to compose myself before I quietly spoke my vows to Carolyn.

1. Wedding Song

Listen to the song of our hearts.

Peace and Joy as we commit to one another.

Rainbows guide our way home

and see the stars

as they shine in the darkness.

Hear the wind Precious One

as it whispers our names.

Feel the warmth of the fire

as it glows in the darkness.

Feel the calm

in the still of this moment.

Close your eyes,

feel the freedom within.

Dance with me

in the wonder of Life

as our hearts beat together.

Horizons of happiness have opened

to see the stars sparkling in our eyes.

Beautifully serene,

lovely as we give vows

to sing our love.

Made magnificent in front of the world.

True Love beyond measure

marking unobtrusive beginnings.

Just as an otter beckons the morning

with a swirl of delight

in a pool of laughter.

You – bring me to awakenings,

wander into my simplicity

to touch and know

and be at peace.

No words of love are ever unspoken

in this wonder of our life.

You were there all along

since before time.

Waiting for me to fully see you

my other half.

Our souls nurtured,

sustaining two pilgrims

gently embraced by song.

Endless horizons of happiness open wide.

2. Where Are You Soul Mate?

Soul mate

are you there my other half?

Awake to your magnificence.

Do you know

that your joy and grace lighten my path?

Do you know

that since I lay with you long ago,

head to head

shoulder to shoulder

hip to hip

and toe to toe in chaste union –

that I have fully known?

You – breaking bread with me

by candlelight

sitting on the floor

by a blazing log fire,

giving yourself to an embrace

mutual and burning.

You – listening as the city wakens

and stretches itself – and wait

for the first footstep

marking unobtrusive beginnings.

Just as an otter beckons the morning

with a swirl of delight

in a pool of laughter.

You – bring me to awakenings,

wander into my simplicity

to touch and know

and be at peace.

No words of love are ever unspoken

in this wonder of our life

You were there all along

since before time.

Waiting for me to fully see you,

my other half.

3. Song of Our River

Embracing sylvan delight,

each curve and eddy of this river

tied to a caress from your body.

I reach to the stars in your hair,

feel gentle, insistent passion in your lips.

Tumbling through rapids,

crowning glory of your hair

cascading through my fingers

into the wonder and awe of you.

In our river of life,

I feel your rhythms through fingertips and stay close.

Your eyes melt all blocks as I draw your beauty

shared through gentle insistence of soft lips.

Swiftly does starlight

run through my spine in the lee of this river.

Steller wonder of your being,

as our river

sings its song.

4. Forest Lakes Remembered

A mantle of leaves

spurred by Autumn's gentle breath,

swift and dance as

I fall silent and at rest.

In the midst of forest lakes

nature leaves her mark.

A heron, blue and stately,

arrogant to all else save his elegance,

looks from his townhouse in the reeds.

Ducks fly away

alarmed at the intrusion.

The leaves are dying yet remain alive – vibrant.

A shimmer of gold as a birch tree speaks

to a rowan so deeply red the sun is put to envy.

I brought you here dear one

to listen to the water ripple

away from a wooden paddle.

5. Dream Song

Sitting – listening.

    Each word resonates within

    the oasis of being

    growing to song.

Dreaming – upon you.

    with my mind tonight

    and last night

    and every night before.

Thought – whispering leaves

    in the wind cast

    snowflakes upon your brow

    slowly melt away

Will – I kiss your lips

    in my mind tonight

    as my heart

    comes quietly home?

6. Dance of the Eyes

Behind a plow of words

a poet writes.

Phrases spiral

as an eagle soars in a sky

with no horizon or meter.

Cascading into passages,

tracing cosmic runes

at the edge of knowing.

Words drift on the morning mist.

A whisper of wind

haunts every thought I breathe.

Enter the Muse –

Waiting, wondrous, so long

for cracks in facades order to crumble,

-     then she grants life to this poem dancing.

Slow pirouette of eyes.

Turning en pointe, knowing glimpses

dancing shared with joy.

Our soft-spoken adoration blows on dandelions

creating parasols drifting to fertile ground.

The waltz of happiness,

exhilaration of vigorous reels

leave all sadness behind –

a funeral march to banish

pain elsewhere.

That was all before our eyes danced together.

My life lives

in each glance of your eyes.

Smiling from you

gently lifting my heart

you reach how deep we bind together.

Connecting where the universe

begins and ends.

Dancing delicate curves of elegant quadrilles.

staccato intensity of flamenco

and the peace of loving serenade.

We dance with our eyes,

cheek to cheek smooch.

All in place,

this dance of our eyes.

The Poetic Voice / Ian Prattis

PART TWO:
Finding My Poetic Voice

During my career as an anthropologist, I was fortunate to encounter many First Nation story-tellers across North America: Dene, Hopi, Ojibwa, Algonquin, Inuit–to mention a few. Their poetic recounting of myths and history had a deep impact on how I thought and wrote.

I would say that without poetry, cultures implode. Indigenous medicine people enhanced my process of remembering the power of the poetic voice. Through their mentoring, I learned how to reconfigure my own understanding of time, place and consciousness. I chose to listen to the sacred feminine voice of Earth Wisdom rather than the multitude of competing voices in my deep unconscious.

I made a radical turn in the 1980s to reconstruct anthropological methodology, as the poetic voice was always required for investigation of the cultural other. I felt that the language of the anthropologist could not represent the raw experience of other cultures.

Furthermore, that poetry is philosophically essential to the work of anthropology. I saw poetry as an uninterrupted process, whereas field notes were not. I suggested to colleagues that the poetry of observation is what anthropologists are supposed to be doing. Anthropologists who commit themselves to poetry in order to say something different about field experience are also the tricksters and shamans of the discipline!

The words "without poetry, cultures implode" leaves the door open for our species and leaders to change. I choose to complete this story with a moment from the focus on *Trees Speaking*. In this poem I criticize human greed and its destructive impulses that result in pollution and contamination of the natural world.

In spite of being exposed to the merciless harshness of the elements, the poet - that is me - still smiles because I am a part of this world, just like a tree or a rock. I see the tabernacle of our collective memory. I harvest these ancient energies and weave them into my own history.

My poetry aims directly for the heart, speaking to the reader in clear and loud words, sometimes screaming the truth. I take a small portion of the epic in order to talk about *Trees Speaking*. The connection between humans and nature is illustrated with a solitary tree and a man. In each other's presence, their feelings of aloneness vanish.

7. Orkidstra

Orkidstra is an Ottawa based development program that empowers music for kids ages 5–18 from under-served communities. Teaching life skills such as teamwork, commitment, respect and pride is the achievement. Orkidstra started in Ottawa with 27 children in 2007 and now includes 700 children and youth, both in-school and after school from over 62 linguistic and cultural backgrounds.

Children from lower-income families receive free instruments and music lessons. It is a social development program that fosters life skills. Tina Fedeski, her husband Gary McMillen and Margaret Tobolowska founded Orkidstra after visiting Venezuela to research El Sistema, where it was established.

El Sistema is a publicly financed, voluntary sector, music-education program founded in 1975 by Venezuelan educator and activist, Jose Antonio Abreu.

Since 1975 El Sistema has used music education as a vehicle for social change. It cultivates an affluence of spirit which brings hope, joy and positive social impact to 400,000 children, their families and communities throughout Venezuela.

This unprecedented success has inspired hundreds of similar programs, estimated at one million children in at least seventy countries around the world. The children become empowered and productive citizens.

El Sistema is an extra-ordinary cultural, educational and social program that pursues the goals of social engagement and youth empowerment through ensemble music education. It has been growing for decades, where children living in impoverished circumstances learn to play and sing in orchestral and choral ensembles. The remaining poems radiate the children in our world.

The Poetic Voice / Ian Prattis

8. Trees Speaking

Whisper of wind through pine needles.

Shimmering aspens and soft poplars of the forest,

a relief to the darkness of the spruce's

darker timbre and twin pronged sheaths.

The river denies our passage

so we walk through sheltered forests

rather than meet

our death by foolishness.

We wander to find herbs, trilliums

white in dense bush,

hiding among the wild strawberries

un-bodied with rich red summer promise.

Guardian trees, lichen laced,

protest the spring violets pushing upwards.

In the forest great many entities

of the earth and sky speak of before

and what is to be.

Clearings sunk into the earth

await further visits.

In the center of one clearing

stood a single tall aspen - lonely.

Waiting for companionship,

fragile in its aloneness,

in her aloneness,

in our aloneness.

I stand within her circle

- this tree and I -

and for a brief moment,

neither were alone.

9. Weaving Autumn in the Canyon

Silver birches silhouette the sky,

gather in numbers quietly.

Elegantly, grace "en pointe,"

sway and breathe

bend and whisper in the canyon.

Leaves shimmer

dancing to gathering wind.

Murmur Creation's tones

in synchrony with stellar rhythms,

their sound carries waves

rolling into shoreline rocks.

Silver birches silhouette the sky.

Light of Sun climbs the sacred canyon

rushing down islands

while shaping Life's meanings.

Sunset fills the sky,

tracing Creator's name

to the rim of eternity.

Right now to every heart,

clouds muster creations

for a cascade of evening.

This symphony of autumn color,

melody from a sky

pastel grey and fiery red.

Descant to the tones

of a painted forest

cooled by lush evergreens.

Sensual beauty, rhapsody of forest, canyon and sunset

fused as a golden sheen.

All caught in a still lake

waiting with patience beyond time and space

to reflect this moment of splendor.

Weaving.

10. Inuit Arctic

An arctic horizon

takes Inuit across the shelf of snow

and frozen sea.

Seeking well known depths of ice

directing his strong dogs,

all ten, that keep them alive.

Together they decide the necessary directions

of their senses and skills

The whip is gently held.

11. Spring Poet

Spring river past

water's loneliness

where nothing grows.

Claws at the stones

with writing not done

to bring poetry to heart light.

Distracted by light

caught in steel bolts

through the ankles not yet dead

ravaged by splinters.

Others mourn to see ashes

dropped into streams of blood

screaming at the violence

of colonial deaths.

12. Storm and Saki

Storm laden harsh day

as wind, rain lash the shore line

restrained by marsh reeds.

The lee in the storm

hurling violence to shake our bones.

We heated saki to give warmth

and take shelter as we

stood

drenched

watching

fearing

slurping saki.

A silence in the storm

before a respite broke the fury

on the spur where our tents were exposed.

The storm forced retreat

to a safer, less exposed haven.

I stand silently in the pine trees

listening to the presence

of the storm's muted whisper.

Feeling their presence.

PART THREE:
Dementia Clouds of Poetry

13. The Buddha's Remembrances

1. Knowing I will get old,

    I breathe in.   Getting old

    Knowing I cannot escape

    old age, I breathe out.   No escape

2. Knowing I will get sick,

    I breathe in.   Getting sick

    Knowing I cannot escape

    sickness, I breathe out.   No escape

3. Knowing I will die,

    I breathe in.   Dying

    Knowing I cannot escape

    death, I breathe out.   No escape

4. Knowing that one day I

    will lose all I hold dear today,

    I breathe in,   Losing all held
                                       dear
    Knowing I cannot escape

    losing all I hold dear today,

    I breathe out.   No escape

5. Knowing that my actions

    are my only true belongings,

    I breathe in.   Actions true
                                       Belongings
    Knowing that I cannot escape

    the consequences of my actions,

    I breathe out.   No escape

6. Determined to live my days

    Mindfully in the present moment,

    I breathe in.   Living mindfully

Experiencing the joy and the

benefit of living mindfully,

I breathe out.   Experiencing joy

7. Offering joy and love each

   day to my loved ones,

   I breathe in.   Offering love

   Easing the pain and suffering

   of my loved ones,

   I breathe out.   Easing suffering

I smiled quietly at the first five stanzas. Then was refreshed by the last two stanzas about living my days offering joy and love to loved ones to alleviate their suffering. The Buddha's Remembrances focused on impermanence – growing old, getting sick, dying, losing loved ones and realizing that my only possessions are the consequences of my actions. The final two stanzas of the meditation show the way – to live mindfully in each moment and offer joy to loved ones. My sharing illustrated that my approach comes through experience, crises, difficulties and joys that may have common ground with many readers. Steadiness, clarity and compassion are within me, rather than ego posturing from the lunatic fringe. It also propels me to serve the planet and humanity by creating bridges and harmony.

14. Demoralized Clouds

Desert legacy gathers

with the desperation of a flower

that talks to the large brown leaves

that shade her.

Delicate petals drop by the wind

and few flowers rarely kiss the earth.

No longer seeking bodies

stretching for the high calla lilies

beside the broken roses.

In spiral depths to name the stars

And leave all grief

with the song of a broken harp.

15. Moving Nightmares

The time between sleep and waking

throughout our bones huddles in dark clusters.

We speak for the dead

feeding ragged moments of fears and sorrows.

We are haunted,

seeking our better selves

in the desert tumbleweed.

Sharing universal shards of memory

breaking through greed and racism,

screaming that our world

is now different.

Black Lives Matter remind us

that we are better

than vague clusters of nightmares.

In a language of nods

to be perfectly understood,

the balmy evening hides moonlit stars,

shimmering through tall pines

from across the river.

His hands shake in the squall of rain,

thinking her fingertips

were placed on the grave of his loved one.

She hears every word he murmurs.

16. Transference

Alchemy faces and warped minds

find wrong memories

about love shrieking beyond.

Just waiting to find perfection

in crows bounding a clear formation

across a fence.

So she believes her death sometime.

Not walking across the steps

to be stopped in a courtyard

with too many knives

grasped in strong gnarled hands

- not hers.

17. The Weirds Tonight

The ancien of Aztec line

carries his lantern

past the weirds

who are hugging trees no less.

He carries his lamp

to feel the earth beneath bare feet

open to stellar wonder

where experience demands.

He has seen it all before,

lifts his lantern in polite salute.

His quiet chuckle

all to himself

shared with the weirds.

The Poetic Voice / Ian Prattis

18. Mote in the Eye

A Greek shepherd sprang to my mind

as I watched rotund Zorba dance

on the tavern floor in Athens.

Remembrance of years past

of sentences, words, ideas exchanged

that sprung between the Greek shepherd and I.

Dust spurned our toes

through olive groves by Epiros

athwart Albania, upon which we pissed

with alacrity to escape the attention

and bullets of border guards.

I learned Greek from him

in that moment of time

as he received English from me.

Two youthful gods in time.

He remembers me, perhaps.

19. Gnarled Autumn

Trees. Dead.

Stretching fingers to the sky in pain.

Waiting for the return,

warmth and renewal long forgotten,

with Winter's graze.

The waning sky casts hues and movement to

stillness in the lake.

Promise of a gentle time during winter's cruelty

- cast aside by buds of torn flowers,

that insist on their dominion.

The evening moon, a delicate mistress sees it all.

Clear diamond light of spring

anticipating the aging leaves left

behind Autumn.

All waiting for the icy hand of Winter

to banish Autumn from the land

20. Culture Revival

Old Indigenous culture,

the edge of the world – forgotten,

should have died,

but did not.

Violence, neglect and hatred

could not kill them.

Their human heart etched in lakes and forests

neglected in a brooding sky setting to a loon's call.

Their canopy of recurrent downpour,

wipes clear the dark oblivion

of how not to be.

How to be human,

they continue.

Old Indigenous culture –

Ojibway, Cree, Haida.

They do that.

21. Stunning Vistas

Threads of centuries

deeply silent journey

awakening stirring

as Gautama became Buddha –

the way for pilgrims.

Shadows creep across

fresh scaped earth

Crows calling loudly.

as black specks of ash.

Depot unknown

my physical death

whose heart leaves the mark.

Stunning vistas

unraveling us all.

Excrement from a cow

to find miracles to crack us open.

The Poetic Voice / Ian Prattis

22. Boots of Snow

Banked softly in the quietness

of dark pines.

The treads of boots

leave prints in the snow.

The trees say very little

in whispered moments

waiting for the Spring surge.

In the middle of the path

a kill-site for Winter

bringing death to a figment at the void.

The echo we cannot hear.

No memory weaves our mind,

Static speaking over media chatter,

then we are broken.

No longer do we speak of seasons.

There is only death

frozen in the forest

without sense of the loss.

We blindly suffer

to roam and rattle in lost realms.

Everything else stretches

articulating crazy shifts.

Oceans are lost to our minds

as we ignore

boot prints in the snow

- All we leave behind.

23.   Dementia

Darkness -

> Casting deep in the arrows sent through the brain.

Elusive –

> Hard to find the words seeking that are needed.

Memory –

> Has many realms that allow one to dig deeply,
>
> whatever arises.

Expressions –

> Of meaning, so others may grasp some new
>
> directions.

Neander –

> Paths help to find what is required – often all
>
> sometimes.

Tumbling –

> Words slide down into a meaning grasp and feel
>
> better.

Insidious –

> Progression into a smile to step forward, carefully.

Anxiety –

> Steps are out, and hopes can exercise to the best,
>
> even if you are the only one there.

PART FOUR:
The Environment
Words with Poetry

The Poetic Voice / Ian Prattis

24. The End of Orca

The oceans are strangled

by plastic upon Orca's passage.

Her pod chokes deathly

garbage starving her calf.

The moon fails Orca,

screaming her worst dreams.

The desolation promoted by empty humans are killing

a sister,

brother,

mother,

with plastic discarded

bringing death to Orca.

Sister Orca does not understand

human betrayal

when her calf drops

to the bottom of the sea.

We are guilty

- only mandated for death

as mere shapeshifters without compassion.

Ancestors beyond our present reach

seek out extinction and silence

- a shrug their only remaining echo.

Can I keep Orca alive

to sustain her complicated Pod?

Listening to the ocean

on the cliffs over the sea,

yearning for their glimpse

and sound from white and black.

She does not need human garbage

....and neither do I.

Humanity is so screwed up!!!!

25. Dead Trees

The trees wait for renewal forgotten.

Autumn merges with Winter's severity,

waning sky casts movement to

stillness in the lake.

Promise of a gentle time,

buds of flowers insist on their dominion.

The evening moon, a delicate mistress, sees it all

anticipating the aging leaves left

behind by Autumn,

shared with Summer's bounty

lay quiet and mantled on trees.

In the rhythm of seasons

the old ones in their later years

notice and calmly carry on

with their private wisdom.

A long wait until man and land renews

in springtime's softness.

Nature's cycle, its rhythm undeterred

as unseen hands speak to us....

26. Ancient Tree

Ancient Tree in Winter

in Canadian waterway,

the reverence of First Nations

cleft by rocks at river's edge.

Water eddies carve your shape

as exquisite sculpture of the forest.

Ice branches creep fingers across the river

as your body disappears under deep laden snow.

Did you stand majestic

as a verdant Rideau River valley?

Were you alone on a high bluff

of thundering rapids

to pull you to their embrace so that you now

lie here trapped, cleft by rocks?

My winter river walk

exquisite beauty for spring's flood

to set you free.

27. Symphony

Let me share it…..

The symphony of autumn color

cascading melody from a sky

pastel grey and fiery red.

Descent to the dancing tones of

a painted forest.

Silver birches silhouette the sky

gather in numbers,

silently, elegantly, grace "en pointe"

and murmur Creation's tones.

In synchrony with stellar rhythms

carries waves rolling into shoreline rocks.

With life shaping meanings –

Right here.

28. Sacred Canyon

Spiral mists descending.

Tree line to shore,

now visible – then gone.

Insistent echoes pierce the clouds

rushing down the sacred canyon

to the rim of eternity

as all our relations know:

> You are here

> With us

> From Before

> > Receive it ….

They weave a tapestry of land, lake and sky.

Eagles of us all.

Mists of time.

break and swirl

wings sweep

full circle in Eagle Creation.

29. The River Claims

My feet slide

without grip

on the ancient cedar

as I plummet into the river.

My lungs gasp to

climb the cold clutch.

To run against rapids

and patient haul

as the First Nations do.

Our passage remains

for necessary threads

with nature's bounty.

Unfinished in my evolving.

The Poetic Voice / Ian Prattis

30. Mill at Chaudiere Falls

The raging falls at Chaudiere slip away,

muscles strain and gasp

to thrust canoe blades deeper

against the rip of piercing eddies.

Boiling current

swings our cedar canoe into a backwater

where the might of industry lay dead.

The pulp mill disused and silent,

still magnificent in decay.

A new beauty filters through its broken arches,

offering a graceful industrial neglect.

An eyrie for pigeons, dead trees, arch and rubble

define the river's cascade over rills of rock.

77

The old mill's disgorge insists forcefully.

Its grip carries the cedar downstream,

past the sculpture of decaying industry.

A disused mill, now dead, provides a burst of mortality,

to know nature's ultimate insistence.

31. Colonial Man

Raised beds in summer

as multi-yellow corn emerges

for a harvest when gentle showers drop

water over leaves.

Indigenous brothers have knowledge

of taking agreements between humans,

earth, creatures and fine air.

Autumn rains cling beneath cedar boughs

and prepare Christmas feasts

-    the careful bounty of harvesting.

But right there is Colonial Man with deadly pesticides

on the earth that burns the Earth.

…. Reciprocation destroyed.

Nothing left for human evolution.

32. Late Refuge

Nothing to keep us warm,

despite dreams stuffed in pockets

where names are never known.

Our hidden oxygen is not used

at the same time a young woman

transpires to make her way, too stubborn to die

behind barricades of fire.

She danced across the road

reflected in the window

of the baker's shop.

Baguettes morph into space

crushed by burdens,

life pauses through tired surrender.

Humanity without knowledge

is why trees cried

over the travesty of barren oil sands.

Trees have a sophisticated internet that

creates majestic forests and fires

as the epiphany of inter-connection.

Cedar forests without pain and desperation

soothe hurts beyond danger

yet required by Mother Earth.

A new tapestry evolves to welcome

the rising up of mountains, forests, oceans

and the return of water creatures.

All intensely watch humanity,

Which, consumes more from the Cedar Forest.

They reach out to homo-sapiens

who cannot see

that animals leave their tracks in the mind.

33. Opening to Killing Our Planet

Trees are smog shrouded 'midst earthquakes breaking.

Conquered violence creates destiny of

our broken planet.

A javelin is thrown into my back,

looking for my heart

afraid of death

Every gift thrown away.

Death everywhere on our planet.

No opening so that every gift is broken.

Seminary of consciousness,

the insistence of crazed abandoned humans.

Other creatures can never come back - ever.

83

Memory cannot find peace monuments

as Death stalks our crippled planet.

PART FIVE:
Footsteps

I met a visiting Rishi to Canada in 1995 – a holy man from India who recognized me and insisted I go to India for spiritual training. I took leave from my university and spent two years as a yogi, where the spiritual treasures of India were opened to me.

In November and December of 1996, I became seriously ill in India. As I observed my bodily systems crashing one by one, I knew there was a distinct possibility of death. I met this with calm and lack of fear, just present with whatever was happening. I was solidly with each moment in a totally timeless way.

I clearly remember Saturday December 21, 1996. as if it were yesterday. On that day I let go of all attachments to my body and surrendered to a sense of freedom never before experienced. I was living in a small ashram in the city of Mumbai – reserved for saints and holy men. I did not qualify for either category yet felt their grace at hand. One humorous manifestation of that grace occurred one morning when I woke up and opened my eyes to greet one of my swami mentors. He smiled broadly and helped me to sit up, then surprised me with his words:

"We are all so happy, Ian, that you have decided to die with us in India, if indeed you are to die. And we will be most happy should you live."

He made me some tea with herbs and beamed love and understanding to me before leaving. When I went to sleep, I was content and happy. I thought about my many mistakes and chose not to deny them or brush aside the bodily pain. I felt all my teachers throughout lifetimes gathering together inside and around me, without boundaries. The next morning to my utter joy. I woke up. Over the next six months I recovered my health and completed my guru training before leaving for Canada.

My work in progress took me back to India six years later. My wife Carolyn and I embarked on a pilgrimage with Shantum Seth – In The Footsteps Of The Buddha – through North India and Nepal in February 2003.

We journeyed to Rajghir, Bodh Gaya, Varanasi, Sarnath, crossed into Nepal at Lumbini and then to Kushinagar, Vaishali and Sravasti. I created poems to provide a glimpse of experiences that are too immense to otherwise communicate. I am not so interested in monuments and old bricks. My wish was to record Living Dharma - people, life and experience in their mundanity. The Footsteps of the Buddha pilgrimage was full of wonder and miracles. It was a journey to the center of being so that everyday life becomes a pilgrimage and whatever reality I am engaged with is also pilgrimage.

Next are some of the insight poems that arose.

34. Where do I stand?

It is about standing

not moving an inch

from there.

Walking, Speaking, Acting.

Making war memorials

into peace monuments

to respect our planet.

Two minutes to midnight

for our fragile planet.

Warriors must transform their lives

is where I stand.

35. Torch Arriving

Oldest son, named for me.

My father's lineage,

Lines strike

the magnificence of your being.

Your father's purpose –

the gate of no escape,

open to universal wonder.

The torch is passed

with kin and people

so that you know

Pilgrim for Peace.

Receive the Torch.

36. Steel Eyes Dying

Steel barrel blue, flint eyed

tears running down his face.

He did not go gently into his magnificence

gripped by all who loved him.

The altar brings the valley

of sunrise to his heart.

The morning mist

rock him slowly to his song.

A gentle new awakening.

He came to the gate of no escape

and opened to his own wonder.

37. Keystones

Coleridge's "Kubla Khan"

a drastic poem of cosmic decisions

and poetic choices.

Death stalks the perimeter

feeding off the hubris of life

lost at the edge.

Yet there is a center

in patient rainbow dreams

full circle as we gather.

> I am a key stone.

My arms encompass all

with joy and love at the center.

> You are a key stone.

Rivers run as we descend to cellular depths

changing rhythms to crystalline,

    We are a key stone.

Life's lucid movements

know if love is renounced

behind locked doors.

The world sinks

into a pit of disaster.

I face both ways

warrior guardian of dawning integrity.

    I am the key stone.

Let death roam taking that of my life

which cares not to dance this dream alive.

Constellations change

bursting shackles and bondage.

You are a key stone.

In the verdant garden

I plant myself in soil resonance

remaining this path

We are the key stones

making choices.

38. Return to Tulum

The selfie sticks clump in swarms

before the monuments of Tulum.

Plastic posterity

right where I sat.

I entered the walled city of Tulum – thirty years ago.

Now sequestered behind ropes and strict security.

The price of graffiti, looting and volley ball.

The ancients could still be heard,

presence emerging with stillness and respect,

though silent to oiled sunbathers.

Whistle blowing security guards usher hooligans

from forbidden ceremonial pyres.

Marching out where they cannot be.

Years past my similar space

was bound with personal reverence.

I whispered registers with Mayan radiance.

The Gods Face All Ways.

A murmur vibrated the five openings

of the walled city and ceremonial center,

misnamed by Juan de Grijalva in 1518.

This majestic monument atop the cliff

crowned a temple

complete with blood-stained sacrificial stone,

sloping steeply to the Caribbean Sea.

I sat in the Upper Temple decades ago

alert to corner-stones facing west.

Masks with mouths wide open. Teeth filed.

Thirty years later a similar stone,

at the foot of the monument

outside the security rope.

I sat upon this stone

placed on the cliff edge

the mesmerizing energy from time before.

Before, I could not put pen to paper.

Now, I can

The Poetic Voice / Ian Prattis

39. Trailing Sky Six Feathers

I wrote in my India diary that a female entity orchestrated all the energies to keep me alive, though I did not understand at the time.

She had an embroidered buckskin tunic, using an eagle feather to brush energy over my body, chanting in unison.

When my grandfather died, I felt him as a tangible presence in his coffin. I quietly whispered, "Go to heaven now Grandpa."

I remember at his wake how upset I was at relatives drinking, arguing and being disrespectful, so I sought my grandmother. She wiped my tears, then walked into the living room of her house and with quiet authority asked everyone to go home. She did not think I was a crazy kid as I cared for my grandfather's death. My leap of faith was understanding about death and dying – merging with the wisdom mind of the universe.

I woke up in Mumbai, India and heard crows saying hello outside the windows. I felt moving along the path of understanding.

40. Moonlight

The moon's veiled fleeting clouds

mysteries of grace

bringing down the stars.

Now bright, now dark.

No sense or reason

casts the moon leaving

with rhythms dancing.

Swift eddies navigate storms.

41. The Otter – An Dhoran

My boat – "An Dhoran" loved the sea

heading home to Barra with tourists.

The sea started to swell

clouds grew black with fierce wind

- my little boat tossed about.

The sea was angry

started to swell

we would all die this day.

I could see lights on every house

as we racked my boat.

The sea was roaring with wildness.

Our hearts leaped along the East Coast

though we could all die this day.

Pulling my boat towards Castlebay road

beneath the stars and lights.

Our little wooden boat was safely home.

We did not die this day.

42. Indigenous Wisdom

Ancient Wisdom beckoning my heartbeat.

Speaking to each drop of sweat

as we paddle away from the city.

Ottawa River – home to First Nations.

Trees dance on last year's leaves

by the river's edge.

The mighty river spoke to the forest

and I listen deeply,

willing to step across the divide of regret.

The river held the threads of before

that keeps Earth beliefs.

Once presence is left, this river becomes our rhythm.

Pacing rapids, knee deep in the river's grip,

the water pulls and threatens our canoe.

Asserting dominion is the way of the river

running through Mother Earth.

Weakened by portages

from the ascent of rapids.

Searching deep for strength

then the wondrous peace of silence

follows by river's edge.

Taking the moment to flow

with this river as she speaks quietly

to our canoe.

PART SIX:
Journey

"See yourself walking through a beautiful meadow, full of flowers. You hear the sounds of insects humming and birds singing. The sun feels warm on your face and a slight breeze ruffles your hair. As you continue walking, look up into an endlessly clear blue sky, and for a moment allow yourself to merge with it and enter such clarity. Three shamans come from the deepest part of yourself and they represent your own powers of creativity and self-healing. The shamans understand and support your presence. Thank them for their support and power of healing.

Their transfer has power to create understanding and

healing for you. The feminine source of earth wisdom is

for your transformation as it discards all damaging.

The feminine source of earth wisdom is the lightning rod

for your transformation. This powerful healer serves you

with infinite depth and force".

Say quickly to yourself 'I have arrived. I am home'."

43. My Poetic Voice

During my teenage expedition to Sarawak, Borneo with Voluntary Service Overseas, I kept a journal of the vivid surrounds and how I was feeling. From that time on I scribbled poetry where I went, accumulating poems that reminded of the experiences.

My extensive shamanic training with incredible First Nations medicine people was also carefully logged. Those notes and poems were a sign-post to always be authentic, even when it was difficult to re-read.

As a professor I wrote text books and scholarly papers that were somewhat stifling. I had to re-learn how to write without sounding pompous.

I had a challenging journey through life. My journey through life navigated shamanic healing of childhood sexual abuse, guru training as well as a near death experience in an ashram in India. My life stretched my attention beyond a novel way and so I wrote twenty poetry and prose books.

My life as a global traveler certainly stretched any limits I could have placed on it. My approach to life comes though experiences, crises, difficulties and common ground. The grittier it became, the harder to maintain relationships.

In my career as a Professor I was fortunate to encounter many First Nation story tellers across North America: Dene, Hopi, Ojibwa. Algonquin, Inuit – to mention a few. Over a period of forty years, extraordinary indigenous medicine people enhanced my process of remembering the power of the poetic voice. Through their mentoring, I learned to reconfigure my understanding of time, place, consciousness and re-write some of Carl Jung's psychology.

I chose to listen to the feminine voice of Earth Wisdom rather than the multitude of competing voices in my deep unconsciousness. The stories I tell in my poetry books are offered as a gift to our planet. We have made our world an unpredictable beast because we fail to work with it intelligently. As I grow into being an elder in my early eighties, I find that I offer responsible stewards to live in harmony.

44. Wolfie

Timber wolf inspected me –

not his natural world.

He was there at the far west of Mt. Currie

in 1990.

Distinctive white markings on head, chest and forelegs.

He moved like a wraith outside my cabin.

My tins of salmon attracted him

as he stealthy grabbed them, then disappeared.

His fur a reddish-brown color.

I turned in to my cabin

and heard him come to the veranda

and settle for the night

leaving fresh strands of his fur.

The cabin door was left open.

Dying embers brought Wolfie by the hearth.

He knew his territory, but

carefully scrutinized me

leaving for a while.

This beautiful creature

had decided to live with me in Eastern Canada.

I arranged for my son, Iain, who lived in Squamish

to pick up Wolfie.

He wondered why on earth I was going

to so much trouble.

I purchased a strong crate in Vancouver

The lone wolf was waiting - patiently.

The journey to Vancouver Airport Cargo

took the wolf to the back of the truck

yet the wolf quickly found the front seat

next to Iain.

Wolfie knew where he was going!

My heritage in Gatineau Forest became his new home.

Wolfie could read my mind.

His loving heart was felt by everyone

and was instrumental in Carolyn's attention

– my wife 34 years ago.

I had met her at ballroom dance class

and asked at the end of a magical evening.

"Would you like to see my wolf?"

I thought she must think this was

the worst pick-up line in history!

But her beautiful green eyes said "Yes."

Wolfie was splendid.

I rolled down the window of my grey Jeep Cherokee.

He placed his large paw gently on her hand.

She fell in love with Wolfie first of all

and decided that anyone who had such a creature

must be special!

So began our wonderful togetherness

of love and marriage

continued with this wonderful creature.

Wolfie was with us until he passed on.

His presence is always with us in every moment.

45. Bodh Gaya

"This is my simple religion. There is no need for temples, no need for complicated philosophy. Our own brain, our own heart is our temple. The philosophy is loving kindness."   Dalai Lama.

Walking pilgrims

trace Gautama's footsteps.

Centuries of quiet walking

-    mere strands of Mother India,

footsteps between pilgrims.

Emaciated Gautama's cave

Yet to receive warmth

from Sujata's grace.

Then with awakening stirring

at Bodh Gaya

Gautama became Buddha,

Asceticism abandoned

for the Middle Way.

Words drift by in the morning mist,

finds every thought one breathes.

Waiting wondrous so long

for façade's order to crumble.

46. Deity Beware

Listen to Deity snarled and

slithered out knocking the door.

I revile all of you

with fire, sarcasm and scream

with inflicted personal pain

until you realize

the steps for Nirvana's crown.

Find the volumes of Verdi's

symphonic echoes

to sing your way to clasp

the direction of Oracle.

Atlas lifted to the stars

to a throne high.

Then no longer bleed anymore.

47. Punk Palace

Moonlight speaks of the morning passing by,

life crises turn beyond wreckable,

preventing boundless life entering grim death.

It makes the stars and galaxies dance

The moon does this.

The gateway to boundless space

is the door to troubles and joy

yet the moon and stars

dance together – beyond any sense or reason.

The sky casts movement and hues

to something we can touch.

The full harvest moons

rise from banks of pastel grey

pacing existence

through the rhythms of the universe.

48. Swept Out Loud

The roar of Orkidstra swept loud by children

is relentless - shadowing by the Muse

understanding to overcome the past.

Finding myself as a healer, mentor

and educator

to find the true nature so that

humanity and the world may

be renewed.

I reach for my backpack

and take out a writing pad

with its gold-plated pen

to tell the story by hand written.

Finding grace, illumination with

wonder and awe.

The man in the flesh, blood and bones

is the receiver and giver

of love to all crossing my path.

The 1X of Pentacles

reflects where I am right now-awake,

serving and grateful.

My narrative goes to extraordinary lengths

to understand.

A learning experience

to stretch beyond myself to new choices.

I am clear with my directions

at this perfect time and way

    -a strong sense of inner peace

    -and security.

I stretch myself beyond my years

To a full and abundant life.

The value of the

journey I have been on.

Every moment

The Poetic Voice / Ian Prattis

49 Finding Trailing Sky

Home at last, preoccupied with memories,

and I questioned Trailing Sky –

"Was it you that brought my boat safely home?"

I already knew the answer.

She was there every time my life was at risk

I affirmed her life guardian presence.

Ater a long pause, she responded,

"I had to keep you alive, your son too

and when you were dying in India."

My dialogue took another level.

"When I finally die, will you be there,

what will happen to you?"

Her voice was firm and precise.

"You changed course with courage and

determination, and went to extraordinary

lengths to erase the karma carried from

childhood."

"When you die, I will be your last moment;

I will guide us as one integrated mind

and leave the path open for Carolyn

when it is time for her death."

50. Epilogue

The song continued never too late for him.

His knowing shocked his people into new awareness.

They were good people of adversity and survival.

He fashioned creativity

by quiet gentle example.

The raw primacy of sea, rock and gale

let them turn

that stretched back to Antiquity.

They came where the young ones started their work.

They looked and measured many things.

Leaving only to return in one's and two's.

The postman trimmed the founds,

carrying cement on his back from the roadside.

His bicycle lay with a wheel spinning in the wind.

A shipwright from the sea laboured on his leave

to put a roof to the place.

They felt the lasting joy of being ensnared by the thread

of life

that ran back to that time before Antiquity

they heard and felt the song rejoicing in their hearts.

51. The Future of War

"I want to talk to you about our children and the kind of future we create for them. Do we teach them peace? Or through neglect do we allow violence to flood their minds, hearts and consciousness so they learn war? Even worse, do they live out our own personal wars expressed through our violent attitudes, speech and actions towards them? I ask every adult, particularly men, to deal with their internal wars so that only the best in us is passed on to our children, not the worst in terms of violence. How do we deal with our internal wars, hatreds and fears that constitute our neglected minds?

We must stop hiding behind addictions and busyness. We come to a stop, look deeply into the eyes of our children and make a commitment to face our internal demons and transform them by stepping on to the path of compassion. Not by transmitting our wars and internal afflictions to the children of the world. We need community to support us in sacred ceremony, meditation and creative spirituality. We must raise our consciousness by retraining our minds, through refining our speech, attitudes and actions. We show our children the way to peace by learning to be it. The level of hate and violence globally has increased dramatically. Excessive violence has been used to create killing. There is no "them" and "us." We either learn to live peacefully together or we all die together.

All violence is injustice and we have to teach our children the truth about war. Not about winners and losers, but about the suffering on both sides. It is only citizens of the world standing together for peace and saying "No to War" that will stop it. But the hatred grows and the suffering increases. What can we do as individuals to change this? We go to work on ourselves. First of all, we uproot the violence and war within our minds. To prevent war we nurture non-violence. We practice meditation and prayer in daily life to transform the poisons within our minds and within our nation.

We enter into true peace negotiations by learning the methods of deep listening, of respectful and non-violent communication. By understanding and bringing our mindless, selfish agendas to a stop. We create peace by knowing that compassion is the antidote to violence and hatred. We must also make peace with Mother

Earth. If we injure Mother Earth, we injure ourselves. Our civilization has caused such deep harm to the earth that we humans may soon become an endangered species.

The solution is not political or economic, these are secondary. The primary solution is spiritual. Every faith and spiritual tradition must renew its ethics and responsibilities and honour the interconnected nature of humanity with Mother Earth. We must make it clear to our political and corporate leaders that the violence they commit in our name is no longer acceptable. We must hold them to account and influence them with our clarity, wisdom and courage. The actions we take now are shaping the possibilities for future generations.

So here is our challenge. Today, in the pouring rain and thunder storms we have experienced peace, a deep peace shared between many traditions, cultures and religions. This experience evaporates into nothing if we do not translate it into action. Begin the work on yourselves today, so that your attitudes, speech and actions become an example to your children, friends and communities. Take the practical steps to make peace with Mother Earth in terms of what you consume and support. Then represent your community, in coalition with other communities, to political and corporate leaders. Show clearly that we are choosing peace and harmony within ourselves, within our communities and with Mother Earth. Together we can do it.

We are Ambassadors of Peace after all."

The Poetic Voice / Ian Prattis

PUBLICATIONS - THE AUTHOR'S WORKS

To the best of my ability, I endeavor to follow Gandhi's principles of *ahimsa* (do not harm) and the teachings on mindfulness. These are the guidelines and foundations for my peace and environmental activism.

I live very simply as a planetary activist, Zen teacher, and recognized guru in India. My initial task is to refine my own consciousness - to be a vehicle to chart an authentic path.

The focus on daily mindfulness enables me to be still and clear. My passion for the preservation of Mother Earth propels me to serve the planet and humanity by creating bridges and pathways of mindfulness for community activism. Over the past fifty years I have penned twenty-one books. My hope is to get your attention!

I have transformed several writings from my prior books to cast a sharper short story more suitable to this collection. I thank respective editors Mark Rossi, Bob Barclay and Michel Weatherall for their belief in my work.

* New Directions in Economic Anthropology. Special Edition of the Canadian Review of Sociology and Anthropology, 1973

* Reflections: The Anthropological Muse
  American Anthropological Association, 1985

* Leadership and Ethics
  RSVK India, May 1997

* Anthropology at the Edge: Essays on Culture,
  Symbol and Consciousness
  University Press of America, 1997

* The Essential Spiral: Ecology and Consciousness
  After 9/11
  University Press of America, 2002

* Failsafe: Saving the Earth From Ourselves
  Manor House Publishing, 2008

* Earth My Body, Water My Blood
  Baico Publishing Inc, 2011

* Song of Silence
  Baico Publishing Inc, 2011

* Portals and Passages: Book 1 and Book 2
  eBooks on Amazon.com Kindle, 2012

*   Keeping Dharma Alive: Volume 1 and Volume 2
    eBooks on Amazon.com Kindle, 2012

*   Redemption
    Xlibris LLC, 2014

*   Trailing Sky Six Feathers: One Man's Journey
    with His Muse
    Xlibris LLC, 2014

*   New Planet New World
    Manor House Publishing, 2016

*   Painting With Words: Poetry for a New Era
    Manor House Publishing, 2018

*   Shattered Earth: Approaching Extinction
    Manor House Publishing, 2019

*   Past, Present and Future: Stories that Haunt
    Manor House Publishing, 2021

*   Four Phases, Lost, Impermanence, Bittersweet,
    Caring
    Manor House Publishing, 2022

* Sacred Ceremony and Desert Legacy
  Manor House Publishing, 2023

* The Poetic Voice
  Manor House Publishing, 2024

* 2 CD's and 2 DVD's

* 4 films

* 8 Professional Honors, 5 book awards

* 10 Scientific and Technical reports

* 200 professional articles/chapters/book reviews
  published

* 26 Electronic television courses broadcast
  at Carleton University TVO

* 50 articles in Pine Gate – Online Buddhist Journal

Manor House
www.manor-house-publishing.com
905-648-4797

The Poetic Voice / Ian Prattis

Manor House
www.manor-house-publishing.com
905-648-4797

www.ingramcontent.com/pod-product-compliance
Lightning Source LLC
Chambersburg PA
CBHW070751120626
46557CB00002B/552